Heartfelt Inspirations

D0004647

Loving Angels

Laurette Therrien

MODUS VIVENDI

© 2002 Les Publications Modus Vivendi Inc.

Publications Modus Vivendi Inc.
3859, Laurentian Autoroute
Laval (Québec)
Canada
H7L 3H7

Layout: Modus Vivendi
Cover Design: Marc Alain

ISBN: 2-89523-105-2

Legal deposit, 4th trimester 2002
Bibliothèque nationale du Québec
Bibliothèque nationale du Canada

Canada We acknowledge the financial support of the Government of Canada through the Book Publishing Industry Development Program (BPIDP) for our publishing activities.

Government of Québec — Tax credit for book publishing—
Administered by SODEC

Heartfelt Inspirations

Loving Angels

Laurette Therrien

MODUS VIVENDI

REFLECTIONS ON ANGELS

Whatever the era, civilization or religion we refer to, human beings have always had special — often intimate — relationships with the world of angels. And if a small percentage of us persists in denying the existence of these beings of light, the great majority prefers hanging on to this belief which allows us to live better, to believe in the eternity, and to hope for a better world.

By calling directly to his or her angel, the individual reaches a degree of understanding that would remain unreachable at the level of earthly conscience, because man is a material being who use his logic, and tends to neglect his spiritual dimension.

Because of that, and because of the weight of the matter he is made up of, man often disregards his intuitive abilities, therefore not allowing himself to communicate with these beings of wisdom that angels are. However, his balance and the world's redemption depend on their influence and the energy they radiate.

Ego limits us. By calling to the celestial mediators that angels are, by trying in every manner to communicate with them, by keeping his ears open to their celestial voices, man, who aspires to harmony, opens himself to a heightened knowledge of the invisible world.

To perceive the subtle messages sent by our angels when we succeed in communicating directly with them, we must be willing to listen and learn, without letting ourselves be limited by the apparent depth of the mystery.

Here are for you some chosen thoughts that will help you reach a state of meditation susceptible of bringing you closer to your angel, while leading you to live in harmony with our earthly world, and the great Beyond.

L. T.

If angels are the thoughts of God, as many believe, there is therefore an infinite number of them to watch over our destinies.

L. T.

Those who understand only what can be explained understand very little.

M. VON EBNER-ESCHENBACH

What we perceive and understand depends on what we are.

HUXLEY

Angels and ministers of grace defend us!

SHAKESPEARE

In the shadow of
an old oak tree
My head on your knees
I dreamed the most
beautiful dream
Filled with sweet angels.

L. T.

Our guardian angels, more trustworthy and
enlightening than all the world's astrologers,
can counsel us on the best way to take for rich
and fruitful lives.

The true seeing is within.

G. ELIOT

In the silky rays of a radiant morning
I opened my eyes and thought I saw an angel
The child was still sleeping... peace, sweetness
and silence.

L. T.

I wanted to talk to the angels, these celestial beings. I tried with all the sincerity I could, and already I felt less alone. Their presence lives inside of me.

L. T.

Everyone must be the assistant-gardener of his own soul (...).

HUYSMANS

Angels are with us wherever we are: at home, in the car, in airplanes, in trains, at work, at the building site. Everywhere, every moment, they are watching over us.

L. T.

The wise one never stops creating.

H. DESBOIS

Little faith is put in them
Whose faith is small.

LAO-TZU

Angels are androgynous beings, they only have
a gender through our perception of them, and
that can vary from one individual to the next.

L. T.

The outer sense alone perceives visible things
and the eye of the heart alone sees the invisi-
ble.

R. OF SAINT-VICTOR

Angel of softness, angel of simplicity
Let me follow your footsteps
I want to go beyond myself.

L. T.

Come the fall with its stormy skies
Come the cold, come the frost
My angel warms my heart
and gives me courage.

L. T.

And the Angel said, "I have learned that every man lives, not through care of himself, but by love."

TOLSTOY

At my mother's bedside, frightened at the thought of a too-slow agony, I saw an angel and I understood that it was there to watch over this beautiful soul that had given me so much.

L. T.

Vision is the art of seeing things invisible.

SWIFT

To love and to be loved
— this
On earth is the highest
bliss.

H. HEINE

When large numbers of people share their joy in common, the happiness of each is greater because each adds fuel to the other's flame.

ST. AUGUSTINE

It is said of angels that they inhabit the interior space, and that they are responsible for the harmonious organization of this uninhabited universe.

L. T.

Everything, by an impulse of its own nature, tends towards its perfection.

DANTE

Angel, my friend, I don't perceive you with my eyes and ears, but in the form of waves or vibrations, your very own way of revealing your presence.

L. T.

An angel is an intelligent being whose presence at our sides reveals itself through different vibrations. Their feelings for us are real, even if they often escape our comprehension.

O! Beautiful azure angel, angel of friendship
Comfort the lonely souls and hearts
Soothe them with softness, grace and forgiveness
Give us this love which leads to peacefulness.

L. T.

Beauty is always bizarre.

BAUDELAIRE

 *Your guardian angel is all love, and if you take the time to talk to it, it listens to you with understanding and indulgence.*

It is said that angels have the faculty of communicating with us on all levels of conscience, respecting each individual's capacity.

It is agreed that an angel is male and female at the same time: it possesses the attributes of both genders according to its own personality and the needs of the individual it is protecting.

Your discreet presence, O! angel, comforts me and fills me with joy. Consciously or unconsciously, I wish for your presence, I am calling you with all my heart every moment of my life.

L. T.

Angels can fly because they take themselves lightly.

G. K. CHESTERTON

Many English expressions refer to angels: to be an angel, to speak of angels, to go where angels fear to tread... Did you also know that a backer for a theatrical production is called an angel?

You wish to get in touch with your angel? Open your heart and your soul to the vibrations that surround you and subtly infiltrate you.

L. T.

Angel of love,
Angle of kindness
Carry my love
Into timelessness.

L. T.

Angels encourage us by guiding us onto a path that will lead to happiness and hope.

LAKEY

The one who speaks to his or her angel does it for a greater personal well-being, of course, but mainly to take part in a better world, what is indispensable and vital.

There are many ways of talking to angels, and all are good; what matters most is to find the way which suits you best.

If they allow us to develop, angels evolve themselves through their contact with us, making this an infinite and infinitely stimulating process.

It is the soul, and nothing else, which allows us to communicate with our angels, when, in the silence of our inner beings, we implore help from above.

L. T.

The poet enters into himself in order to create; the contemplative enters into God in order to be created.

T. MERTON

Whether or not we believe in angels, they are among us. And by speaking to them, we can improve our lot and walk, confident, towards a more luminous destiny.

The word "angel", from the Greek angelo, means messenger. And in the case of angels, the message is limpid: love, love, love.

L. T.

My angel's breath kept me light as a feather in the wind. My angel is an angel, it is nothing fantastical.

L. T.

Contact with an angel is good: good for the human body and soul, of course, but also good for the energy that circulates in the universe and the cosmos.

After Herod died, an angel of the Lord appeared in a dream to Joseph in Egypt and said, "Get up, take the child and his mother and go to the land of Israel, for those who were trying to take the child's life are dead."

THE BIBLE

There was a pause – just long enough for an angel to pass, flying slowly.

R. FIRBANK

The awe of God is wisdom.

HESCHEL

A dove landed on my windowsill, quiet and white
It was my beloved angel, at last revealed.

L. T.

The child, in his cradle, dreams
Graceful and confident
And smiles... to the angels, assuredly.

L. T.

As there is much beast and some devil in man, so is there some angel and some God in him.

COLERIDGE

As knowledge increases, wonder deepens.

MORGAN

I was feeling about me a scintillating presence
When I heard it sing, then whisper
Fascinated, abandoned, I let myself be soothed
By the angel of serenity.

L. T.

Paintbrush in hand, short of inspiration
Suddenly I felt a muse inspire me with the idea
At once, I knew it was the angel of creativity.

If you haven't forgiven yourself something, how can you forgive others?

D. HUERTA

Among angelical creatures, there are, they say, the spirits of nature, better known as fairies, sylphids, salamanders, trolls, gnomes, elves.

They say, of a skilfully-made work of art, that it came from "the hands of fairies". And that may be true since the artist is inspired by the angel of creativity.

Nowadays, people are more likely to say: "to be born under a lucky star," but in the end, it is the same since angels, more particularly Thrones and Cherubs, watch over the stars and planets.

L. T.

Jacob (. . .) dreamed that there was a ladder set up on the earth, and the top of it reached to heaven; and behold, the angels of God were ascending and descending on it!

THE BIBLE

At 92, my little aunt Rose is an angel: she is filled with angelic thoughts, and when we come near her, unconditional love touches us.

A cherub was walking on the tip of his toes, his little diffuse body leaping as if pushed by a cloud.

L. T.

Believe in something larger than yourself.

BUSH

In my hand, a September flower
On my lips, a tender song
And to fly away, the wings of an angel.

L. T.

Stoop, angels, hither from the skies!
There is no holier spot of ground
Than where defeated valor lies,
By mourning beauty crowned!

H. TIMROD

In the sweet-smelling flower garden
I felt in my neck something like fluttering wings
It was a blue angel, breathing in all the scents
Of the eternal beauties.

L. T.

Every hour of the day, whatever activity I am involved in, my angel watches over me and comforts me, when doubt or anguish disturb my peace of mind.

Believing in angels is not unreasonable if we think that those who believe in angels must first believe in man.

I saw the tracks of angels in the earth,
The beauty of heaven walking by itself on the world.

PETRARCH

The virtue of angels is that they cannot deteriorate; their flaw is that they cannot improve. Man's flaw is that he can deteriorate; and his virtue is that he can improve.

THE TALMUD

The soul's immortality is a possibility to which no one is impervious. And to shed some light on this matter, it is good to consult the angels.

How should we address angels? Simple: by singing, dancing, smiling, stopping in the street to talk to the homeless... because angels are wherever there is kindness.

Have you never heard the angels' whisper?
Like water in the river, it flows and sings
A quiet whisper, for those who know how to listen...

L. T.

Let your holy Angel have charge concerning us,
that the wicked one have no power over us.

M. LUTHER

Angels protect children and watch
over grownups
They are pure spirits; gifts from heaven
That have come to guide us without blinding us.

L. T.

God is as close to you as
your thoughts allow him to
be.

SRA DAYA MATA

If we value the pursuit of knowledge, we must be free to follow wherever that search may lead us.

STEVENSON

When your heart opens up
When your soul is at peace
You welcome the angel
and your fears fade away.

L. T.

Wise men hear and see
As little children do.

LAO-TZU

When I am happy, I think of my angel, and every time I feel its presence, I notice an intensification of my happiness. Its approval is very dear to me.

L. T.

Awaking with a start at the end of a terrible nightmare, at once I felt enveloped by immense and warm wings protecting me. Ever since then, I have believed in angels...

It is a sad thing to think that nature speaks and that humankind does not listen.

V. HUGO

If you ever dreamed of flying, you may have identified with the angels, and you believe you know how it feels to have wings.

L. T.

Angels sow wisdom and faith and help us look at life with eyes filled with understanding and tolerance.

Beauty is a gift, gentleness a virtue; my angel possesses both, and its presence comforts me in difficult times.

L. T.

A shiver runs down your spine when you realise it is not our imagination. Something is watching us out there.

S. BURNHAM

God provides thread for the work begun.

J. HOWELL

I work with children who are innocent and without malice, but who need to be watched over relentlessly; the task is huge, but I am not alone, a flock of angels are swarming around them, and mine, every instant, is supporting me.

L. T.

I often feel I do not love enough, and in those times, I have doubts about myself, about others, about life. When doubt is so overpowering that it stops me from going forward, I call my angel who helps me recover lightness of heart.

There are those who give with joy, and that joy is their reward.

K. GIBRAN

Friendship, I understood a long time ago, is a gift from Heaven. And when my friends are gathered in my home, smiling and faithful, I feel surrounded by angels, and I thank Heaven for it.

L. T.

Some things have to be believed to be seen.

R. HODGSON

 *Generosity is a quality of the heart that we sometimes lack in difficult times when selfishness has a tendency to take over.*

Every day, each human being meets barriers he must cross. Life is extremely demanding. Opportunities to surpass oneself being numerous, we must know how to call to angels for guidance.

L. T.

I want to be an angel,
And with the angels stand
A crown upon my forehead
A harp within my hand.

U. LOCKE BAILEY

A mystery is something that falls in with doubt and gradual unveiling; so it goes for angels who govern our lives: there is need of much patience and faith to be at last certain of their presence.

L. T.

As a flickering flame advancing in the night
I saw the angel of mercy float on towards
   a friend
Its singing voice filled the air
And hope was revived inside my moved soul.

L. T.

The golden moments in the stream of life rush past us and we see nothing but sand; the angels come to visit us, and we only know them when they are gone.

G. ELIOT

No one is so good that another may not be just as good.

SAYING

Angels help us distinguish between what should be loved, therefore worthy of love, and what should not, because unworthy.

A thing of beauty is a joy forever.

KEATS

*Nature is but a name for an effect,
Whose cause is God.*

W. COWPER

*Between the palpable and the impalpable,
between the celestial universe and the earthly
universe, angels are the condition of reality for
all and the proof that all coexists.*

*To reveal themselves, angels appeal to our senses.
You could feel a breath of air in your ear; a
pressing on your shoulder; a light touch of your
hand... All you have to do is be attentive to
notice signs of their presence.*

L. T.

To be good is noble, but to show others how to be good is nobler and no trouble.

TWAIN

We are each of us angels with only one wing. And we can only fly by embracing each other.

L. DE CRESCENZO

Angels are remarkably fluid, which makes them flexible beings capable of wrapping us in their divine essence.

Angels are invisible? Not for those who open wide the eyes of their hearts and live their spirituality day by day.

L. T.

*There can be no true good-
ness nor true love without
the utmost clear-sighted-
ness.*

CAMUS

*The energy coming from angels is not physical,
meaning it is not transmittable through a palpable body; angelic energy is metaphysical, supernatural.*

*There are brilliant works, that of Mozart, of
Michelangelo and many others, which are so
transcendent that they lead us to believe that
they were inspired, if not totally dictated by
angels.*

L. T.

*There are some cold and hard beauties we asso-
ciate with the powers of evil; and there are
suave and soft beauties we readily associate
with angels; they can share the same traits, but
the eyes seldom deceive: that is where we can
read the soul's worth.*

Search for truth in contemplation and not con-
tinuously in mouldy books. He who wants to see
the moon looks up at the sky and not at the pond.

PERSIAN PROVERB

In the eyes of children
Blue eyes, brown eyes,
grey eyes, green eyes
In the eyes of children,
are hidden the most beautiful angels.

L. T.

If a man is not rising upwards to be an angel,
depend upon it, he is sinking downward to be a
devil.

COLERIDGE

Thrice he assayed, and thrice,
in spite of scorn
Tears, such as angels weep,
burst forth.

MILTON

Awaken first by yourself, then look for a master.

CHAN PROVERB

O! my angel, you who knows me more than anyone
Intercede on my behalf with the Eternal
Be my protector, my guide and my hope.

L. T.

If we refer to all the ancient writings of the great religions, we understand that angels are the masters of space and time and that the workings of the universe depend on them.

At the end of forty days and nights in the desert, Jesus, having resisted Satan's temptation, was surrounded by angels who came to attend him.

THE BIBLE

Angels are the indispensable link that fills the gap between God and earthly creatures; they are our mediators with the Almighty.

L. T.

The finger of God was on me all day — nothing else could have saved me.

DUKE OF WELLINGTON

Guardian angels are our representatives; they intercede for us with the Eternal and plead the cause of men, it is part of their mission.

L. T.

For thousands of years, Jews have believed that there is some kind of magic emanating from the names of angels, who, according to the superstition, confer on them spiritual energy and knowledge.

When we are in love, what we want more than anything else in the world, is to stay in love. The same goes for angels, those who have come into contact with them but once wish most of all to continue communicating with them, as they are love itself.

L. T.

The more materialistic science becomes, the more angels I shall paint. Their wings are my protest in favor of the immortality of the soul.

BURNE-JONES

The highest wisdom is kindness.

THE TALMUD

Some maintain that the existence of angels, their presence among men is the irrefutable proof that the Kingdom of God is near.

It is sometimes hard to overcome one's anger, especially when injustice and hate take over. In these moments of helplessness in the face of human folly, it is good to be able to turn to these beings of kindness, sent to comfort us.

L. T.

It is not enough to do good; one must do it in a good way.

CONDORCET

Angels are men of a superior kind;
Angels are men in lighter habit clad.

YOUNG

We are such stuff as dreams are made on...

SHAKESPEARE

The stars are in the sky to remind mortals the objective they must aim for.

CHINESE PROVERB

An angel is an intelligent essence, always in motion. It has free will, is incorporeal, serves God, and has been bestowed with immortality. Only the Creator understands its true nature.

ST. JOHN OF DAMASCUS

If the cosmic order reflects the heavenly order, then it is fitting that the angels' universe be parallel to ours, but at a higher level of spirituality.

The spirit of the wise one is the mirror of the sky and earth, in which all things are reflected.

TCHUANG-TSEU

If angels sometimes appear in the human form, the supernatural light shrouding them transfigures them to the point where it is difficult, for a human being, to look them in the eye.

All things speak of God.

YOUNG

If sex is everywhere, love is rare. While accepting that love and couples are simply human, we can turn to angels to reach the absolute in love.

L. T.

Four angels to my bed.
Four angels round my head,
One to watch, and one to pray,
And two to bear my soul away.

T. ADY

A finger points at the moon. Too bad for the one who only sees the finger.

OLD SAYING

Thousands of candles can be lighted from a single candle, and the life of the candle will not be shortened. Happiness never decreases by being shared.

BUDDHA

Think, in mounting higher,
The angels would press on us, and aspire
To drop some golden orb of perfect song
Into our deep, dear silence.

E. BARRETT

Angelic natures understand that great souls, endowed with generosity and capable of respect, and not the most beautiful and best shaped people, offer true and sincere love.

L. T.

How beautiful, how great
How majestic they are, these angels of light
Come to accompany me at the end of a long
journey.

L. T.

While you are searching for your neighbour's
faults, how will you rejoice from the invisible
world's beauty?

AL-DÎN ATTAR

I called to my father, he had left us
I called to passion, it had withered away
I called to my angel, I found eternity.

L. T.

Beauty is eternity
contemplating itself
in a mirror. But you
are eternity and you
are the mirror.

K. GIBRAN

By doing good, we become good.

ROUSSEAU

I am the Angel of the Sun
Whose flaming wheels began to run
When God's almighty breath
Said to the darkness and the Night
Let there be light! and there was light.

LONGFELLOW

When I go through difficult times; when times
appear dark and obstacles impossible to clear, I
simply turn to my kind angel, who restores my
courage and lightness of heart.

According to the Scriptures, angels were created
long before the stars and mankind. These spiritual
beings were here well before us, therefore
angels are not deceased people come to watch
over us, as some would believe.

L. T.

Inspiration comes to me when I think of archangels
Who trace the destiny of thousands of human beings
Inspiration comes to me when I invoke angels
And when I think of you I met on this crossing.

L. T.

To call to angels, we only need a little humility and faith. The people who recognise that they cannot control and do everything by themselves, communicate more easily with angels.

Angels are intelligent reflections of light, that original light which has no beginning. They can illuminate.

ST. JOHN OF DAMASCUS

Archangel Ariel,
lion among lions
Prince of the rivers
and of the seas
Drive away for us
the demons of pollution.

 *Angels are an inexhaustible source of pure energy, and even without acknowledging them, they guide us and accompany us in the most important moments of our lives.*

Even if our angels reveal themselves spontaneously, in precise moments of our lives, we must sometimes call to them to benefit from their benevolence.

Pay attention, because angels can appear in different forms, according to the time and place: sometimes a beam of light, sometimes flickering light, they can also appear in the guise of an old man or a child, of a friend or a stranger.

L. T.

And since you are a breath in God's sphere and a leaf in God's forest, you too must rest in reason and move in passion.

K. GIBRAN

To come into contact with angels, we must trust our vibratory abilities. But they often appear on their own, when we are going through troubled times and wish for better lives.

Beware: we can try to make contact with our angels, but we cannot dictate to them what to do, or incite them to act according to our will. Simply ask for their protection.

All which liveth tendeth to good.

EMERSON

Under a willow,
in the botanical garden
I heard angels
singing hymns
To the glory of heaven
watching over the flowers
For our pleasure to behold.

L. T.

Faith leads us beyond ourselves. It leads us directly to God.

POPE JOHN PAUL II

When Clara was born, in the middle of the night, an ineffable light flooded the room. Exhausted, but delighted, her mother understood that Clara was not alone, that her kind angel was there to facilitate her entry into this world.

Angels help us recognize happiness in life's small things. Their simplicity and gentleness lead us on the way to the truth of all things.

Your angel is there for you, but it can also benefit the people you love. Do not hesitate to ask your kind angel to watch over your children, your parents, your friends, when they are in need.

L. T.

We shall find peace. We shall hear the angels, we shall see the sky sparkling with diamonds.

CHEKHOV

For I truly had seen angels, and they had ministered unto me. And also, I had heard the voice of the Lord speaking unto me in very word, from time to time...

EXCERPT FROM THE BOOK OF MORMON

Peter was a solitary and silent little boy. At the park, he liked to play alone in the sandbox, and moved away every time another child came near. "I'm not alone," he said to his nanny who wanted him to make some friends, "I'm with my angel."

L. T.

O! Uriel, angel of fire, angel of light, help me attain clarity and illumination, today and all the days to come.

When you feel you are stagnating in your spiritual development, address the archangel Michael so he will help you continue walking in wisdom and grace.

I sometimes ask myself, when I feel a sudden burst of affection towards another human being I hardly know, if it is not the angel, in him, who inspires me such an emotion.

L. T.

When you stop in your activities to meditate, make sure to call the divine angels to your side, so they can accompany you on your journey to your superior self.

Every time I see a rainbow, rich with all the colours of the prism and of all shades, I cannot help but think of angels, to which we attribute the same beauty, the same luminosity and the same lightness.

L. T.

When my angel is present, when I feel it watching over me, then my love and gratitude for all that surrounds me overflows, and I understand that compassion is the most beautiful virtue in the world.

L. T.

If there is something that keeps the mind open to angel visits, and repels the ministry to evil, it is pure human love.

N. P. WILLIS

People who get the chance to see angels say that they felt infinite love, immeasurable tenderness, and an incomparable sense of well-being.

The sun was bombarding us with its rays when I felt covered with love. Dazzled by the light and soothed by the warmth of that wonderful summer, I understood that angels were also celebrating that day.

L. T.

When you hurt too much, physically or morally, turn to the angel Raphael, the divine healer, so he can help you overcome the difficulties that are paralysing you and keeping you from going on.

Did you ever ask yourself if there was some supernatural force pushing you to do certain things instead of others when you rely on your intuition?

My angel is so discreet, it is so unassuming, that sometimes I don't recognise him: yet, it reveals itself all the time, through a voice's softness, through the eyes of a child, through the hand that stops me from crossing the street when there is danger ahead.

L. T.

All God's creatures are His family; and he is the most beloved of God who does most good to God's creatures.

MOHAMMED

My God sent his angel and shut the lion's mouths and they have not hurt me, because I was found blameless before him.

THE BIBLE

To overcome your fear of living, your fear of loving and being loved, call to Gabriel, the angel of divine force, so he can help you surpass yourself and overcome your fears and weaknesses.

*So that love stays with you always
Make a lot of room inside
To welcome the angel of happiness.*

L. T.

Few persons have courage to appear as good as they really are.

J. C. HARE

 *O! Angel Raphael, you whose name signifies healing, relieve the world and all its creatures from the terrible hardships we inflict on them because of ignorance or desire to possess.*

The things that are unseen are eternal.

THE BIBLE

And behold, many did declare unto the people that they had seen angels and had conversed with them; and thus they had told them things of God, and of his righteousness.

EXCERPT FROM THE BOOK OF MORMON

Angel Melchisedech, great sage and king of Salem, who took human form to teach the power of faith and redemption, direct the light, as you did in times long ago, on this distraught world where violence and chaos rule.

And what keeps us from believing, as some maintain, that we have more than one angel? There are tens, hundreds and thousands of them watching over us, in turn when necessary. They say we only need to let them come to us.

Our certainty that angels right now witness how we are walking through life should mightily influence the decisions we make. God is watching, and His angels are interested spectators too.

GRAHAM

Man is neither angel or beast; and the misfortune is that he who would act the angel acts the beast.

PASCAL

Upon the surface of a motionless lake, on this luminous May morning, I saw a light angel skating, its wings spread open.

L. T.

I am a little world made cunningly
Of elements and angelic sprite.

DONNE

O! You invisible messenger
You who watches over my children,
my brothers and my loves
Cover them with your wings,
help them overcome their troubles.

L. T.

The sphere was white and extraordinarily luminous, I walked in its direction, and I found myself in an enchanted space where everything was bathed in God's infinite love.

TESTIMONY

There were three of them, three white, luminous and quiet figures, swirling around over our heads, while we were diverting on the raging river, peaceful, confident, unaware of the danger.

TESTIMONY

The measure of love is compassion; the measure of compassion is kindness.

ANONYMOUS

Sing for us, angel Israfel
Sing the greatness of the heavens and of creation
May your magnificent voice soothe our passions.

I didn't see it, I only felt its hand rest on my shoulder at the moment when I was about to throw myself out into the void. At once, I understood that I wasn't alone and that my life was precious.

TESTIMONY

 *To Christians, Gabriel is the angel of divine power, the one to whom God gave the most important missions on earth, like the announcement to Mary.*

The wind was blowing really hard that day, and Macha was in a hurry to go back home before the storm, when a swirling light appeared and forced her to slow down. Lifting her head to see what was happening, she saw, incredulously, an angel smiling down on her.

TESTIMONY

Disciples of Islam consider the angel Gabriel to be the spirit of truth, and according to the belief, it is he who inspired the Koran to the prophet.

L. T.

In the Jewish legend, it is the archangel Gabriel who ordered the Red Sea to part, so that the Israelites could escape from the pharaoh's soldiers.

I was coming out of a torrid and unhealthy love affair, and I was sinking into depression, when the angel revealed itself. As soon as I saw the halo of light emanating from it, I felt soothed, comforted. After its visit, resentment and bitterness had left me.

TESTIMONY

The quality of contact we can have with our angels depends largely on each person's spiritual level. Indeed, a certain availability of the spirit is necessary to perceive the presence of a spiritual entity.

L. T.

Angels are our true and trustworthy servants, performing offices and works that one poor miserable mendicant would be ashamed to do for another.

M. LUTHER

Seeing is believing all the world over.

CERVANTES

What good shall I do today? What good have I done today?

FRANKLIN

Joseph Smith, the author of the Book of Mormon, tells about the apparition of the angel Moroni: "I called again upon the Lord and he shewed unto me a heavenly vision. For behold an angel of the Lord came and stood before me. It was by night and he called me by name and he said the Lord had forgiven me my sins."

EXCERPT FROM THE BOOK OF MORMON

Thank you life, for sending me an angel
Thank you for the kindness, thank you for the warmth
Thank you for the light of day and the taste of oranges
Thank you life, thank you, I am in heaven...

The clouds are the dust of his feet.

NAHUM

A certain Monroe, after having experienced an encounter with an entity, maintains that "our angel is the part of ourselves which keeps the memories of our past lives"; and so "an encounter with an angel would be an encounter with yourself," he says.

TESTIMONY

What if we talked of the angels' charm?
What if we talked of this freedom
*   emanating from them*
This freedom they give us,
to simply be happy.

L. T.

I have an angel and I am delighted
I am no longer alone on Sundays
or on Mondays, or on Thursdays
I will never be alone again,
this is why I am smiling at you.

Now cracks a noble heart.
Good night sweet prince:
And flights of angels sing
thee to thy rest!

SHAKESPEARE

Nothing is so firmly believed as what is least known.

MONTAIGNE

The first time I left my baby with a babysitter, he was three months old. When he saw me come back at night, after a long day of absence, his eyes lit up and he started giggling irrepressibly... The angel of life was passing by.

L. T.

In the midst of my fears, it revealed itself
I felt its warmth, its glory, its beauty
Reach all the way to my heart, for eternity.

L. T.

God always has an angel of help for those who are willing to do their duty.

T. L. CUYLER

Children are God's apostles, day by day
Sent forth to preach of love, and hope, and
peace.

J. R. LOWELL

To live in a state of grace, is to live accompanied
You only have to believe, you only have to hope
Loneliness does not exist, angels are always there
For the believers.

We were made men and not angels in order that
we might seek our happiness through the medi-
um of this life.

M. DE UNAMUNO

There was morning, there
was evening, there was night
There is the beauty of the
flowers in my garden
And the presence of an angel
in the hollow of my hand.

L. T.

In heaven an angel is nobody in particular.

SHAW

In a dark time, the eye begins to see.

T. ROETHKE

Reputation is what men and women think of us, Character is what God and the angels know of us.

T. PAINE

"This is my angel," the little boy said to his mother, come to pick him up at the park. The mother, amused, does not see her child's angel, to whom she holds out her right hand; but at once, she feels a shiver run through her left hand, and in front of her delighted little boy, she says: "Hello, angel, are you coming home?"

L. T.

I feel that I am not alone
I see life as an eternity
As long as there are birds and butterflies
As long as in the smallest flower
angels reveal themselves
I will never be alone,
because doubt has left me.

L. T.

God fills the universe just as the soul fills the body of man.

THE TALMUD

Life would be strange if there were no angels
But there are thousands of them on our journey down here
They are to be pitied, those who doubt they appear.

Believe that you may understand.

ST. AUGUSTINE

I saw them with my bodily eyes as clearly as I see you. And when they departed, I used to weep and wish they would take me with them.

JOAN OF ARC

Time is man's angel.

F. SCHILLER

My faith is brightest in the midst of impenetrable darkness.

GANDHI

Rebellion roars when we tell ourselves there is no justice. And yet, there are the just... my angel tells me, who reads my mind and comforts me with his great wisdom.

L. T.

The Angel that presided o'er my birth
Said, "Little creature, formed of joy and mirth,
Go love without the help of any thing on earth."

BLAKE

Do not fear calling to your angel, as they say
that they radiate infinite love and know how to
comfort us and reassure us only by being present.

L. T.

The angel of light and the angel of darkness are
to wrestle on the bridge of the abyss. Which of
the two shall hurl down the other?

V. HUGO

The main use we make of
our love for truth is to
convince ourselves that
what we love is true.

P. NICOLE

There is no excellent beauty that hath not some strangeness in the proportion.

BACON

If you wish success in life, make perseverance your bosom friend, experience your wise counsellor, caution your elder brother, and hope your guardian angel.

J. ADDISON

To do good without ulterior motive is a generous and almost divine thing in itself.

F. GUICCIARDINI

He who has fed a stranger may have fed an Angel.

THE TALMUD

Death is the beginning of immortality.

ROBESPIERRE

Hope is an act of faith.

PROUST

Heaven, my love, sent you to me
If you are not an angel you are its messenger
And I will cherish you for eternity.

L. T.

When the moonbeam came to
rest on the last flower peaking
out from under the first snow, I
heard an angel whispered to
me: "Hope."

L. T.

Look homeward Angel now and melt with ruth.

MILTON

It must be recess in heaven if St. Peter is letting his angels out.

Z. N. HURSTON

The beauty that addresses itself to the eyes is only the spell of the moment; the eye of the body is not always that of the soul.

SAND

My soul, like a spark of transcendent life, communicates with my angel who breathes hope and comfort into it.

L. T.

If better were within, better would come out.

T. FULLER

Everything is simpler than you think and at the same time more complex than you imagine.

GOETHE

Like love when it is pure
Compassion is a virtue
practiced by angels.

L. T.

Silence is the lan-
guage of God.

S. SIVANANDA

Every visible thing in this world is put in the charge of an Angel.

St. Augustine

Nothing is farther than Earth from Heaven; nothing is nearer than Heaven to Earth.

C. Hare

All we know of what they do above, is that they are happy, and that they love.

E. Waller

And by came an Angel who had a bright key,
And he open'd the coffins and set them all free;
Then down a green plain leaping, laughing,
    they run,
And wash in a river, and shine in the sun.

Blake

The two angels arrived at Sodom in the evening, and Lot was sitting in the gateway of the city. When he saw them, he got up to meet them and bowed down with his face to the ground.

THE BIBLE

The art of painting is only the art of expressing the invisible through the visible.

FROMENTIN

*Your angel is love, faith, and hope
Everywhere it goes, it soothes suffering,
anguish, and remorse
Your angel is love, keep on hoping.*

L. T.

When angels drop on our hearts the sparks of their unconditional love, we are at last overcome with jubilation and joy.

Conscience is God present in man.

V. HUGO

If I can stop one Heart from breaking
I shall not live in vain.
If I can ease one Life the Aching
Or cool one Pain
Or help one fainting Robin
Unto his Nest again
I shall not live in Vain.

DICKINSON

God has given us a world that nothing but our own folly keeps from being a paradise.

SHAW

With these angelic eyes
No one can resist
Gabriel, the magnificent angel
Is love and felicity.

L. T.

Certain thoughts are prayers. There are moments when, whatever the attitude of the body is, the soul is on its knees.

V. HUGO

Angels we have heard on high,
Sweetly singing o'er the plains
And the mountains in reply
Echoing their joyous strains.
Gloria, In Excelsius Deo
Gloria, In Excelsius Deo

Shepherd why this jubilee,
Why your joyous strains prolong
What the gladsome tidings be,
Which inspire your heavenly song?
Gloria, In Excelsius Deo
Gloria, In Excelsius Deo

Beauty is life when life unveils her holy face.

K. GIBRAN

Some claim that we are God's toys; that He plays, through the angels he sends us, at showing the extent of his power and his love...

Oh! those magnificent Christmas hymns... how beautiful they are and how they succeed, every year, in filling us with emotion, immersing us again in childhood and reverence.

L. T.

*All that we see or seem
Is but a dream within a dream.*

POE

According to testimonies, angels, even when they take on the appearance of great and powerful men, have a "feminine aspect" to them. But most of them apparently have no defined gender.

How do you know if an angel has crossed your path? Sometimes you don't, because angels often appear as coincidences.

G. KINNAMAN

I know that if I want to, I can see my angel; I will gaze upon him with my own eyes; I will see him as he sees me.

L. T.

Lullaby, and good night,
You're your mother's delight,
Shining angels beside
My darling abide.

LULLABY

The expression "to discuss how many angels can sit on the head of a pin" means to engage in protracted wrangling, or split hairs.

L. T.

For thou hast made him a little lower than the angels, and hast crowned him with glory and honour.

THE BIBLE

In the case of those who are making progress from good to better, the good angel touches the soul gently, lightly, sweetly, as a drop of water enters a sponge.

ST. IGNATIUS OF LOYOLA

It is not righteousness that you turn your faces east or west; but it is righteous to believe Allah and the Last Day, and the Angels and the Book and the messengers.

THE KORAN

Angel of peace, angel of love
See to it that the wars and conflicts
Plaguing our world
Lead to more wisdom, peace and tolerance.

L. T.

We not only live among men, but there are airy hosts, blessed spectators, sympathetic lookers-on, that see and know and appreciate our thoughts and feelings and acts.

H. W. BEECHER

If you could keep your heart in amazement before the daily miracles of your life, your pain would seem no less wonderful than your joy.

K. GIBRAN

In grade school, I was chosen to play the role of an angel around the Nativity scene. Oh! how proud I was to wear those little white wings. Yes, I can say it now, I was literally floating!

L. T.

The spiritual life does not lead us away from the world but leads us deeper into it.

H. NOUWEN

When we are overcome by some evil will, should we not tremble before the presence of the choirs of angels that surround us?

ST. HILARY

*Aunt Rose always wished to die in her bed
A believer, she had discussed it with the angels
Who were there, that night, among her children,
Invisible, but soothing.*

L. T.

When they had gone, an angel of the Lord appeared to Joseph in a dream. "Get up," he said, "take the child and his mother and escape to Egypt. Stay there until I tell you, for Herod is going to search for the child to kill him."

THE BIBLE

As long as people have bodies, we do not care much about their souls.

ANONYMOUS

One day, my grandmother told me: "You must assume the angel that's inside of you." I was only eleven years old and did not quite understand what she meant. I am still searching for the significance of this enigmatic phrase, and I hope to find it before I die.

L. T.

We do not want wealth. We want peace and love.

INDIAN WISDOM

When Joseph woke up, he did what the angel of the Lord had commanded him and took Mary home as his wife. But he had no union with her until she gave birth to a son. And he gave him the name Jesus.

THE BIBLE

So in a voice, so in a shapeless flame, Angels affect us oft, and worshipped be.

DONNE

Be an angel to someone else whenever you can, as a way of thanking God for the help your angel has given you.

E. E. FREEMAN

An angel of the Lord appeared to him in a dream and said, "Joseph son of David, do not be afraid to take Mary home as your wife, because what is conceived in her is from the Holy Spirit."

THE BIBLE

When in an animated conversation an awkward and prolonged silence occurs, we say, in a whisper as much as possible: "An angel is going by."

Love is oxygen. Love inspires all of the world's beauties.

There is a sort of gratification in doing good which makes us rejoice in ourselves.

MONTAIGNE

But I have stilled and quieted my soul; like a weaned child with its mother, like a weaned child is my soul within me.

THE BIBLE

A chorus of heavenly voices was repeating Gloria
Heaven was jubilant, all was joyous
As the whole universe was singing Halleluiah.

L. T.

Be peace in the storm.

H. DESBOIS

When it is said that a person "works like an angel," it means he or she does things to perfection.

In my most pleasant dreams, those in which I fly, I don't have any wings, but a concentration capacity that is so great, it allows me to rise up above the crowd.

If we live truly, we shall see truly.

EMERSON

I like to think that angels are where I wait for them: in the light's reflection over the quiver on the lake, at the hour when the sun is setting; in the waterfall cascading down onto the rock eroded by the years; in your deep blue eyes where I sometimes get lost...

L. T.

Charles Péguy, a French humanist writer killed in action in 1914, under suspicion by the Church whose conservatism he denounced, said he had a very mischievous guardian angel. "He's craftier than I am... he's got incredible tricks...," he maintained.

It is only with the heart that one can see rightly; what is essential is invisible to the eye.

A. DE SAINT-EXUPÉRY

For every soul, there is a guardian watching it.

THE KORAN

What know we of the Blest above but that they sing, and that they love?

WORDSWORTH

The sixth angel sounded his trumpet, and I heard a voice coming from the horns of the golden altar that is before God.

THE BIBLE

Around our pillows golden ladders rise,
And up and down the skies,
With winged sandals shod,
The angels come, and go, the Messengers of God

R. H. STODDARD

Angels are like rainbows
Intangible and diaphanous
They truly exist
But we cannot always see them.

L. T.

Angels who stayed true to God have the mission of welcoming souls into the beyond and assigning them a place in the heavenly order.

The greatest souls are capable of the greatest vices, as well as the greatest virtues.

DESCARTES

Satan, Lucifer, the fallen angel, head of the rebellious angels, represents the death of the soul, the absence of spiritual life. Rejected, in exile on earth, he remains immortal and tries to conquer the world by destroying it.

A lot was said about the often paradoxical sense of humour angels have when they communicate with their protégés by telepathy. Many pleasantly make fun of the scepticism and incredulity of humans.

An angel is like you, Kate, and you are like an angel.

SHAKESPEARE

I perfectly understand, said God, that people make examinations of conscience. It's an excellent exercise. One must not overstep the mark.

PÉGUY

There the angel of the Lord appeared to him in flames of fire from within a bush. Moses saw that though the bush was on fire it did not burn up. (. . .) At this, Moses hid his face, because he was afraid to look at God.

THE BIBLE

We call "theophany" the appearance of a divinity and the manifestation of the sole God in the Bible; while "angelophany" is an angelic manifestation, generally accompanied by a dazzling light.

Of all the historical figures, Joan of Arc is certainly the most surprising. A small peasant, guided by "her voices," she was able to convince the king and the army that she was endowed with a divine mission.

The one who was later called "the Maid of Orléans" talked about "her voices", and her fervour was so communicative that she crowned the king, despite her youth, the fact that she was a woman, and her total lack of political knowledge.

In myths and dreams, flying expresses a desire of sublimation, a search for inner harmony, a surpassing of conflicts.

EXCERPT FROM DICTIONNAIRE
DES SYMBOLES, SEGHERS

It is at night that it is beautiful to believe in light.

E. ROSTAND

Angels always inspired artists, particularly painters, who, in these mysterious beings, found representatives of God for men, an inexhaustible source of inspiration.

Walk around in museums and see the multiple angel representations that are there. The bronze sculptures with majestic wings spread are especially impressive.

Walk around in cemeteries also. You will see many angel figures on graves and epitaphs. This goes to show the importance of angels in all cultures and religions.

One can ask who, God or man, invented angels. As those intermediate beings seem to float between two worlds, sometimes emissaries of One, sometimes protectors of the other.

Botticelli, for example, painted several of them. In his painting "Mystic Nativity" (National Gallery, London), done in 1500, we can see at least twenty angels around the nativity scene.

L. T.

Must we really associate angels with beauty and beauty with angels? What can we say, then, about all those people who haven't been blessed by nature, aesthetically speaking? Do we have the right to judge people solely on beauty? Isn't that the devil's temptation?

You shall know the truth and the truth shall set you free.

THE BIBLE

To refrain from those reveries where my soul softens and wanders is a constant renunciation.

L. CONAN

May the Archangel Raphael accompany us along the way, and may we return to our homes in peace, joy, and health.

CATHOLIC PRAYER

We have been so long in a downward spin. The angels are calling us up. We are meant to fly and with our spirits we can.

WILLIAMSON

An angel of light has the mission to personify God for us, poor mortals, maybe because the sight of God himself would be unbearable: a bedazzlement.

Met the angel of the wind; I followed its gusts.
Met the angel of the sun; it spoke in my ear.
Met the angel of time; no more after, no more before.

L. T.

We often notice, on the face of a person who is about to die, an incredible expression of serenity, even if that person is suffering from the worst pains. The meeting with an angel could explain this surprising serenity at the time of death.

We sometimes say, and often without thinking: "Miraculously, I didn't go..." or "By some miracle, I didn't listen to him..." The miracle would be, if we rely on testimonies, the intercession of an angel on our behalves.

It must be affirmed that angels and everything existing, except God, were made by God.

St. Thomas Aquinas

The highest point of philosophy is to be both wise and simple; this is the angelic life.

ST. JOHN CHRYSOSTOM

The angelfish is a saltwater fish (squaloid) with a large head and large pectoral fins. It can measure up to two meters in length, and has a form halfway between the ray and the shark.

Friends are angels who lift us to our feet when our wings have trouble remembering how to fly.

ANONYMOUS

Have no fear, Cupid is watching over us.
My little angel, are you not mine?
Oh, I see you like me well enough:
You blush when I look at you.

T. DE VIAU

Cupid, with a soft flame
Breaking open the night of this valley,
Put before Apollon's eyes,
The boy whose soul he had...

T. DE VIAU

Soon my Angel came again:
I was arm'd, he came in vain;
For the time of youth was fled,
And grey hairs were on my head

BLAKE

My angel,—his name is Freedom,—
Choose him to be your king;
He shall cut pathways east and west,
And fend you with his wing.

EMERSON

A work of art is the
means of a soul.

M. BARRÈS

Angels fly around me; I feel them, I feel their light wings vibrating, I know they are frolicking while keeping me company, because yesterday, love bedazzled me.

L. T.

You need a lot of pride to think you are an angel; but you need a lot of humility to finally resemble one.

ANONYMOUS

Angels do find us in our hour of need.

HUFFMAN

When I was young, I had a little angel who talked to me in gestures, and who was quite shameful; later, without my noticing it, it changes a lot: it started talking, wouldn't stop dictating, from my slightest movement to my remotest idea; it behaved much better and was less of a scatterbrain... How bored I was!

L. T.

Whether in the night and in solitude,
Whether in the street, and among the multitude,
Her ghost, while dancing, walks
Like a flaming Torch.

Sometimes it speaks, and says:
*   "I am Beautiful and I demand.*
That for the Love of ME, you love Beauty alone.
I am the Guardian Angel,
*   The Muse, and the Madonna."*

BAUDELAIRE

A   fair   assembly   of   the   female   kind:
A   train   less   fair,   as   ancient   fathers   tell,
Seduced   the   sons   of   heaven   to   rebel.
I   pass   their   form,   and   every   charming   grace;
Less   than   an   angel   would   their   worth   debase

J. DRYDEN

The body is not real,
the soul is. The body
is ashes, the soul is
flame.

V. HUGO

If you hold a flower in your hand and really look at it, this flower becomes your world for a moment.

G. O'KEEFFE

You will find a star to light your way.

EXCERPT FROM UN COURS DE MIRACLES

He who, after being negligent, becomes vigilant, illuminates the earth like the moon emerging from the clouds.

BUDDHA

Life is a flower that lives inside of us, a flower with roots that reach deep within us. We need to nurture it day after day.

H. DESBOIS

When we talk about angels, we cannot allow ourselves to forget Lucifer, the fallen angel. He tries to influence us, but is a bad counsellor and wants to discredit us in the face of God.

The angel, dignified, will never take advantage of the creature it is protecting. The angel is the being's dignity, his greatness and his salvation.

L. T.

To be born tall or short,
poor or rich, what does it matter?
(. . .) Greatness and possessions
are borrowed from Fate;
How we enter into this world,
is how we must leave it.

P. Mathieu

What angel wakes me from my flow'ry bed?

Shakespeare

Serenity is a garden we must tend to each day.

H. DESBOIS

This is too much: I am a human being! Only an angel can forget such a blow, and only a devil can compensate enough for it!

F. GRILLPARZER

The soul has illusions as the bird has wings: it is supported by them.

V. HUGO

The children, amazed,
  watched as the blue tits
Were flying into the flower bushes
Radiant and luminous,
  the birds were chasing angels.

L.T.

I think that a mother is the closest thing to an angel on earth. I see how she is devoted and how she loves unconditionally and I am moved.

J.-P. ROBILLARD

Stone walls do not a prison make,
Nor iron bars a cage;
Minds innocent and quiet take
That for an hermitage;
If I have freedom in my love
And in my soul am free,
Angels alone, that soar above,
Enjoy such liberty.

R. LOVELACE

He who lives in peace with himself lives in peace with the universe.

M. AURÈLE

Thought is the work of the intellect, reverie is its self-indulgence.

V. HUGO

The white lily
Lives each moment
Without a motion.

H. DESBOIS

She was good as she was fair,
None — none on earth above her!
As pure in thought as angels are:
To know her was to love her.

S. ROGERS

People cannot change the truth. The truth changes people.

D. BAIRD

Only a shower of love can make life blossom in all its fullness.

E. HUBBARD

I took my dying mother in my arms an I told her: "I love you, mom, you can let go now." At this, I felt her leave to join the angels.

ALAIN

What you create inside of yourself always reflects outside of yourself. That is the law of the universe.

S. GAWAIN

Nothing reflects better people's souls than the frame in which they live.

A. PARIZEAU

The body is the dwelling of our soul. Should we not take care of the dwelling so it doesn't fall in ruins?

P. JADAEUS

Nature has some perfections to show that it is the image of God, and some defects to show that it is only his image.

PASCAL

When I hit bottom and I was convinced that my life had no more meaning, my angel came to visit me in my dreams and told me this: "Marc, do not forget, you are loved!"

M. POITRAS

It's wonderful to climb the liquid mountains of the sky. Behind me and before me is God and I have no fears.

H. KELLER

Don't forget that each cloud, however black it may be, always has a sunny side facing the sky.

W. WEBER

Follow your heart so your face will shine forth during your lifetime.

EGYPTIAN WISDOM

Beware not to embellish your house more than your soul; take care mostly of the spiritual dwelling.

J. HUS

The spirit is the one who does good or bad, who makes happy or unhappy, rich or poor.

E. SPENSER

Do some good for your body so your soul will want to stay.

INDIAN PROVERB

Only a look, the beginning of a smile are needed to create a first path towards someone else's heart.

H. DESBOIS

Where do angels get this adorable indulgence, this ineffable compassion for weaknesses they cannot comprehend?

L. CONAN

The angel of the Lord also said to her: "You are now with child and you will have a son. You shall name him Ishmael, for the Lord has heard of your misery."

THE BIBLE

Forgive many things, forget some of them.

V. HUGO

Nothing is small to a great spirit.

A. C. DOYLE

The soul finds its rest in little sleep, the heart in few worries, and the tongue in silence.

PLATO

Blossomed the lovely stars, the forget-me-nots of the angels.

LONGFELLOW

The real mosque is the one built deep inside the soul.

ARAB PROVERB

In the culinary arts, angels-on-horseback are oysters with lard served on toast.

The Iranian prophet Zarathushtra had visions: a being of light sometimes appeared to bring him up to heaven, where he could converse with the Almighty, who entrusted him with his mission on earth.

Hush, my dear, lie still and slumber! Holy angels guard thy bed! Heavenly blessings without number Gently falling on thy head.

WATTS

One morning, while making the bed, I found a little white feather. Of course, I told myself it had escaped from the pillow, but it made me smile... angelically.

L.T.

According to the scriptures, angels, these pure spirits, are beings endowed with a luminous intelligence; they are strong and light, and travel boundless distances to accomplish their missions.

"Great dreams", meaning dreams where the forces of Nature appear to us — earth, water, sun, fire – could be manifestations of divine power, a type of annunciation.

Could we forbear dispute and practise love,
We should agree as angels do above.

WALLER

Outside the open window, the morning air is all awash with angels.

*Some are in bed-sheets,
some are in blouses,
Some are in smocks:
but truly there they are.*

WILBUR

*Whether I flie with angels, fall with dust,
Thy hands made both, and I am there:
Thy power and love, my love and trust
Make one place ev'rywhere.*

HERBERT

*There is enough light for those who only want to
see, and enough darkness for those with the
opposite disposition.*

PASCAL

My soul has its secret, my life has its mystery.

A.-F. ARVERS

To "be an angel" means to be sweet, patient, and good. The more I see you, my love, the more I know you are an angel.

There is a silence of the body and of the soul : it is the condition to well-being.

M. TOESCA

Real happiness is in the peace of the soul and of the heart.

C. NODIER

In the twilight, silence is still the best inter- preter of souls.

P. JAVOR

People who act like angels ought to have angels to deal with.

RICHARDSON

Hands are the man, as wings are the bird.

G. NOUVEAU

It is not because angels are holier than men or devils that makes them angels, but because they do not expect holiness from one another, but from God only.

BLAKE

Religion is proportional to all sorts of minds. (. . .) The most educated go all the way back to the beginning of the world. Angels see it even better, and from farther back.

PASCAL

A great soul rises above insults, injustice, pain, mockery; and it would be invulnerable if it did not suffer out of compassion.

LA BRUYÈRE

Pride ruined the angels,
Their shame them restores;
And the joy that is sweetest
Lurks in stings of remorse.

EMERSON

People who have seen the light from the beyond by coming close to death are unanimous: they felt absolute peace, were filled by a feeling of security and gentleness they had never known before.

L. T.

The unconscious manoeuvres of a pure soul are even more remarkable than the schemes of vice.

R. RADIGUET

Heaven is not on earth, but there are pieces of it here. There is on earth a broken paradise.

J. RENARD

It is by listening to our hearts that we will get closer to the angels. It is by letting our hearts speak that we will perceive these celestial beings deployed in a parallel universe.

L. T.

He who lives in truth has nothing to fear.

H. DESBOIS

Patience doesn't always help, but impatience never does.

RUSSIAN SAYING

Old age brings a lucidity youth is incapable of, and a serenity that is much preferable to passion.

M. JOUHENDEAU

Then the woman went to her husband and told him, "A man of God came to me. He looked like an angel of God, very awesome. I didn't ask him where he came from, and he didn't tell me his name."

THE BIBLE

Souls are God's thoughts.

G. DE NERVAL

The peace of the soul comes from moderation in pleasure.

DEMOCRITUS

Though women are angels, yet wedlock's the devil.

BYRON

… But in these wild regions, the soul finds pleasure in sinking into a sea of forests, to glide over the abyss of cataracts, to meditate on the shores of lakes and rivers, and, as it were, to find itself alone before God.

CHATEAUBRIAND

According to Pierre Jovanovic, men are individualists for whom the conviction of "having" a guardian angel is more comforting than the idea of God.

Our lives, and more specifically the lives of the souls living inside of us, therefore do not end at the time of our physical deaths. The heart stops beating, while the soul travels into the beyond towards the Light.

L. T.

... But, what am I saying, God?
Forgive my transports;
It's enough that faith
shows to the eyes of my soul
What a little whiteness
hides from the eyes of my body.

GOMBERVILLE

How many souls truly alive in this swarming of
human beings?

L. BLOY

Luck, coincidence, foreboding... asking questions
about these troubling events that make us avoid
the worst is allowed. We can be tempted to
deduce that a supernatural force is protecting us.

L. T.

A little hardness befits
great souls well.

CORNEILLE

"Wisdom leads us to childhood," said Pascal. And what if childhood lead back to angels?

We have all known someone, who appeared to us during difficult times in our lives, like angels put on our paths to protect and guide us.

According to testimonies, angels do not always have wings, quite the contrary, and yet they travel at the speed of thought. But what makes them act?

Devoting oneself, helping others requires qualities. We often speak of "calling" when we meet people with such generosity, and we tend to say that they are angels.

L. T.

There are many women who are part angel and like to watch over their loved ones; many even voluntarily give their time to better the life quality of their fellow creatures.

Those who have led serious studies on the existence of angels were forced to admit that the latter are divine aids, webs of light through which God transmits his infinite and unconditional love to men.

L. T.

Manoah inquired of the angel of the Lord , "What is your name, so that we may honour you when your word comes true?" He replied, "Why do you ask my name? It is beyond understanding."

THE BIBLE

Death is the beginning of immortality.

ROBESPIERRE

For Christians, encountering something incredible is a chance to believe.

MONTAIGNE

Whether the angels play only Bach praising God, I am not quite sure. I am sure, however, that en famille they play Mozart.

BARTH

One day, on the highway, I thought I had seen a wounded bird, and so I stopped. It was nothing but a piece of white cardboard. I immediately went back behind the wheel, and two kilometres later, the car that was following me before I stopped hit a huge moose. The driver was killed on the spot.

L. T.

My God sent his angel, and he shut the mouths of the lions. They have not hurt me, because I was found innocent in his sight. Nor have I ever done any wrong before you, O king.

THE BIBLE

The angel answered, "I am Gabriel. I stand in the presence of God, and I have been sent to speak to you and to tell you this good news. And now you will be silent and not able to speak until the day this happens, because you did not believe my words, which will come true at their proper time."

THE BIBLE

God speaks, we must answer him.
The only fortune I have left in this world
Is to have sometimes wept.

MUSSET

Why does the idea of meeting an angel seem so strange to us? Maybe because the angel is sent by God and we still doubt this mysterious presence.

Great souls are always prepared to turn hardships into virtues.

BALZAC

We sell the thrones of angels for a short and turbulent pleasure.

EMERSON

The image of the understanding, gentle mother devoted to her children in each step of their lives is still very much fixed in our Judeo-Christian societies. Of course, this angelic mother is an ideal few can reach, although many aspire to it.

Behind all happiness; behind all joy
Behind all happy adventures
There is an angel watching over us and showing us the way.

L. T.

For fools rush in where angels fear to tread.

POPE

He who overcomes will, like them, be dressed in white. I will never blot out his name from the book of life, but will acknowledge his name before my Father and his angels.

THE BIBLE

Uriel is part of the four superior archangels in charge of ensuring justice. "Fire of God" in Hebrew, Uriel is the angel most cited in the oriental liturgy.

"Being an angel is strange, said the angel." No, I cannot write that, Prévert did it before me, but the temptation to take over his verse is great, they are so simple and so beautiful!

L. T.

Our souls have more capacity for pleasure than for pain.

DE BIRAN

*Struggle against yourself,
you will gain peace of the
soul.*

*An angel, going by
Gestured for me to follow him
Without hesitating an instant
I spread my wings...*

L. T.

*According to Valery Larbaud, each country has
its guardian angel, presiding over everything,
from the inhabitants' beauty to the state's ;
Larbaud called it "the geographical angel".*

*I always thought that if I met it, I would recog-
nize my angel by its wings, but what if it doesn't
have any? Oh, yes... that light!*

L. T.

She speaks!
O, speak again, bright angel, for thou art
As glorious to this night, being o'er my head,
As is a wingèd messenger of heaven ...

SHAKESPEARE

The angel supposedly has no definite form or sex. It is rather an extraordinary light, a "pure flow of energy" which has no voice or wings, but which communicates telepathically and moves the same way, at a breathtaking speed.

Let us keep our spirits free, it is the only peace of mind, the real one, the only real one.

C. JASMIN

Beyond lies
Rests the truth
Its roots dive
Into the heart of simplicity
To each the task of finding it.

H. DESBOIS

Hate, like love, feeds on the smallest things.

BALZAC

Love is peace and trust.

T. TARDIF

The archangel Michael appears as the angel of Yahweh, his Hebrew name means "who is like God". Prince of angels, he must confront the devil in a historical fight. He comes to the help of the Jewish people.

The garden flew round with the angel,
The angel flew round with the clouds,
And the clouds flew round
and the clouds flew round
And the clouds flew round
with the clouds.

W. STEVENS

Blessed are those who heal us of our self-loathing. Of all the services that can be rendered to man, I know none more precious.

W. H. WHITE

Human beings, by changing the interior attitudes of their spirits, can transform the exterior aspects of their lives.

W. JAMES

*I put it in my pocket
To bring it everywhere
It's my pocket-size angel
A wonderful asset.*

L. T.

There is peace only between spirit and spirit.
ALAIN

True happiness is not found in any other reward than that of being united with God.

MERTON

Consideration like an angel came
And whipped th' offending Adam out of him.

SHAKESPEARE

And so Tom awoke and we rose in the dark
And got with our bags & our brushes to work.
Tho' the morning was cold,
    Tom was happy and warm,
So if all do their duty, they need not fear harm.
And the Angel told Tom if he'd be a good boy,
He'd have God for his father and never want joy.

BLAKE

Don't you have, Lord, enough angels in heaven?

HUGO

We cannot leave from the infinite, we can go there.

J. LACHELIER

Angels watch over Nature, over the sun and the rain, over the fertility of members of all species. Angels are mediators between God and men who want to resemble him.

An angel has no memory.

T. SOUTHERN

No rules for great souls: they are for people who only possess the talent we acquire.

DELACROIX

Strong spirits are not jealous or fearful: jealousy is doubt, fear is belittlement.

BALZAC

Mary stood weeping outside the tomb, and as she wept she stooped to look into the tomb; and she saw two angels in white, sitting where the body of Jesus had lain, one at the head and one at the feet.

THE BIBLE

He who binds to himself a joy
Doth the winged life destroy;
But he who kisses joy as it flies
Lives in eternity's sun rise.

BLAKE

I have more memories than if I were a thousand years old.

BAUDELAIRE

No joy equals that of helping others.

SAI BABA

See that you do not look down on one of these little ones. For I tell you that their angels in heaven always see the face of my Father in heaven.

THE BIBLE

There was a violent earthquake, for an angel of the Lord came down from heaven (. . .). His appearance was like lightning, and his clothes were white as snow. (. . .) The angel said to the women, "Do not be afraid, for I know that you are looking for Jesus, who was crucified. He is not here; he has risen, just as he said."

THE BIBLE

Return, return to the infinite, it alone is big enough for man.

LACORDAIRE

To trust, to hope
It's the angels' secret
That one of them
  whispered to me.

L. T.

For the Son of man is going to come in his Father's glory with his angels, and then he will reward each person according to what he has done.

THE BIBLE

Angels may be very excellent sort of folk in their own way, but we, poor mortals in our present state, would probably find them precious slow company.

J. K. JÉRÔME

In the Apocalypse, Gabriel is presented to us as the angel interpreter of visions and prophecies, his Hebrew name means "strength of God".

In the Gospel according to Luke, Gabriel announces the birth of John the Baptist to Zachary. In the Koran, he reveals to Mohammed his calling as a prophet. Catholics celebrate him, like Raphael, on September 29th.

*The world is blind
Rare are those who see.*

BUDDHA

When I paint a friend's portrait, I can't resist the urge to draw him wings. Big or small, white or pink, they make everyone smile; I even believe wings subtly transform them.

L. T.

The earth is to the sun what man is to the angel.

V. HUGO

Raphael, one of the "seven angels who stand before God", was Tobias' protector and healer. His Hebrew name means "God heals"; he is celebrated on September 29th.

I awoke, and my body shuddered violently, and my soul was so troubled that it fainted. But the angel who had come and talked with me held me and strengthened me and set me on my feet.

THE BIBLE

When the Son of man comes in his glory, and all the angels with him, then he will sit on his glorious throne. Before him will be gathered all the nations, and he will separate them one from another as a shepherd separates the sheep from the goats.

THE BIBLE

An angel came by yesterday in my room
It sat in the fringed armchair
Hummed a tune, unhooked a cloud
It was the most beautiful angel, it had your face.

L. T.

I Heard an Angel

I heard an Angel singing
When the day was springing,
"Mercy, Pity, Peace
Is the world's release."
Thus he sung all day
Over the new mown hay,
Till the sun went down
And haycocks looked brown.
I heard a Devil curse
Over the heath and the furze,
"Mercy could be no more,
If there was nobody poor,
And pity no more could be,
If all were as happy as we."
At his curse the sun went down,
And the heavens gave a frown.
Down pour'd the heavy rain
Over the new reap'd grain ...
And Miseries' increase
Is Mercy, Pity, Peace.

BLAKE

 *Among the Archangels, the most well-known are Gabriel, Michael, Raphael, and Uriel; it is said that they can be distinguished from the other angels as they are angels of light.*

I throw myself down in my chamber, and I call in, and invite God, and his Angels thither, and when they are there, I neglect God and his Angels, for the noise of a fly, for the rattling of a coach, for the whining of a door.

DONNE

The work of the whole world has a hundred times more art, order, proportion and symmetry than all of men's most industrious works. It would therefore be hard-headed blindness not to recognize the almighty hand that shaped the universe.

FÉNELON

In a great soul, everything is great.

PASCAL

Angelology experts agree to say that guardian angels are our fellow travellers on earth. They reveal themselves when we appeal to them, quite simply.

A shivering, the sound of a wing
I barely felt a feather brush against me
An angel had just gone by...

L. T.

Peter was sleeping between two soldiers, (. . .) and behold, an angel of the Lord appeared, and a light shone in the cell; and he struck Peter on the side and woke him, saying, "Get up quickly." And the chains fell off his hands.

THE BIBLE

Men should be mourned for when they are born, not when they die.

MONTESQUIEU

Man is a pendulum oscillating from beast to angel.

V. HUGO

We want to be immortal, and to achieve it, God sent us these spiritual beings whose infinite goodness illuminates winged eyes.

L. T.

Abraham put forth his hand, and took the knife to slay his son. But the angel of the Lord called to him from heaven, and said, "Abraham, Abraham! (. . .) Do not lay your hand on the lad or do anything to him; for now I know that you fear God..."

THE BIBLE

One of Botticelli's contemporaries, Andrea Del Sarto painted "The Sacrifice of Abraham," where we can see a cherub holding back Abraham's arm as he is about to sacrifice his son Isaac.

The worst things generally come from the best that have gone awry. Devils come from angels.

L. T.

Instinctively, we know that these celestial and diaphanous beings love us unconditionally, that they are there to counsel us, protect us and make us forget our torments.

L. T.

A woman with a lover is an angel, a woman with two lovers is a monster, a woman with three lovers is a woman.

V. HUGO

The sun, and death, cannot be looked at fixedly.

LA ROCHEFOUCAULD

And beware lest you lift up your eyes to heaven, and when you see the sun and the moon and the stars, all the host of heaven, you be drawn away and worship them and serve them, things which the LORD your God has allotted to all the peoples under the whole heaven.

THE BIBLE

We sometimes hear it said about certain children that they have "seraphic" airs, which means that they radiate extreme sweetness, that they have the naivety and innocence of angels.

I love the clouds... the clouds going by... over there... the wonderful clouds.

BAUDELAIRE

Virtues can diffuse massive quantities of divine and spiritual energy.

Among angels, there are three hierarchies, divided into three choruses:
Seraphim, Cherubim, and Thrones;
Dominions, Virtues, and Powers;
Principalities, Archangels, and Angels.

Seraphim are celestial beings who surround the throne of God, singing the music of the spheres, and regulating the movement of the heavens.

Thrones are the companions of the planets, and for us down here, the important thing is to recognise the Earth angel, who watches over our world.

Dominions, although they seldom make contact with human beings, intervene to facilitate the integration of the material world with the spiritual world.

And what's above is in the past
As sure as all the angels are.

STEVENS

Who did you give your heart to?
Do not tell me you took it back.
Do not, my love, leave me this way
And come kiss me, angel, I beg of you.

L. T.

Unless a beautiful woman is an angel, her husband is the unhappiest of men.

ROUSSEAU

It seems that people who were declared "clinically dead" came out of their bodies, and saw themselves literally "floating" above the beds where they lied.

Men are trainee angels.

V. HUGO

There is an angel in the Family who, by the mysterious influence of grace, of sweetness, and of love, renders the fulfilment of duties less wearisome, sorrows less bitter.

G. MAZZINI

In the face of true love, human beings tend to say "I met an angel."

Letting angels go by without waving at them would be a serious mistake for those who want to rise above the fray.

L. T.

If men were angels, no government would be necessary.

J. MADISON

The angels are so enamoured of the language that is spoken in heaven, that they will not distort their lips with the hissing and unmusical dialects of men, but speak their own, whether there be any who understand it or not.

EMERSON

Did you ever get this strange feeling that you were "protected" by something impalpable, inexplicable, but whose reassuring presence you felt very strongly?

L. T.

Cherubs are the guardians of the stars and the light. The divine light they diffuse from heaven is reflected on all our lives.

What angels invented these splendid ornaments, these rich conveniences, this ocean of air above, this ocean of water beneath, this firmament of earth between? this zodiac of lights, this tent of dropping clouds, this striped coat of climates, this fourfold year?

EMERSON

Enjoy the Spring of Love and Youth,
To some good angel leave the rest;
For Time will teach thee soon the truth,
There are no birds in last year's nest!

LONGFELLOW

To give, to receive, to share
That is what angels teach us
When we stop and pay attention

L. T.

Every time you hear a bell ring, it means that some angel's just got his wings.

F. GOODRICH

I know the strange
Variety of black
That is called light.

E. GUILLEVIC

What surprises me, said God, is hope. And I cannot believe it. This little hope that looks like nothing at all. This little girl hope. Immortal.

PÉGUY

When muses amuse themselves by making us waltz, the angels accompany them with their celestial harps. Let us celebrate Sundays, let us dance in elation.

L. T.

Men cover the devils they are with the nicest angels they can find.

M. D'ANGOULÊME

Revere beauty, but do not forget to beware of it, because they say that behind the delicacy of its features, a fallen angel may be hiding...

L. T.

*Pure angels, radiant angels
Carry my soul into the heart of heaven!*

CARRÉ AND BARBIER

*Lightness is sweet to the heart that suffered
The feather is lifted by the slightest movement
And love elevates us to the paradise of lovers.*

L. T.

The guardian angel, it would seem, is not always on the shoulder of the individual it is protecting, but sometimes covers him like a cope.

Privileged people who, on the fringe of death, met their angels, felt they were enveloped in unconditional love, a love that radiated from the beings of light accompanying them.

Still an angel appear to each lover beside,
But still be a woman to you.

T. PARNELL

The sky is, over the roof,
So blue, so peaceful!

VERLAINE

Truly, truly, I say to you, you will see heaven opened, and the angels of God ascending and descending upon the Son of man.

THE BIBLE

According to E. Swedenbord, an English philosopher of the XVIIIth century, angels are souls that chose Heaven; one of them needs but to think of another angel for that angel to immediately appear.

Desire and pain cannot disassociate themselves
Nor love and gentleness
To believe in eternity.

L. T.

For he will give his angels charge of you to guard you in all your ways.
On their hands they will bear you up, lest you dash your foot against a stone.

THE BIBLE

Angels have no gender, since they live forever.

A. COMTE

There are those who are closest to God, the Seraphs, the Cherubs, and the Thrones, pure spirits, diaphanous, and disembodied, that none of the world's ugliness could ever reach.

Inspiration is an answered prayer
An angel leaning on the poet's shoulder
When words jostle each other before finally coming together.

L. T.

There are also these majestic guardian angels with their huge wings spread, the picture of the greatest wisdom, whose sole presence seems to soothe all suffering.

The desire of power in excess caused the angels to fall; the desire of knowledge in excess caused man to fall.

BACON

"Angelism" is the expression for a desire of extreme purity, a tendency to believe of oneself as being disembodied, to act like a pure spirit.

Cherubs are often depicted bodiless, floating in the air with a pretty head of curly hair adorned with pink and golden wings covered with light down.

Angels we believe in are omnipresent, they hear our prayers and share our most intimate secrets. They know our true desires, and are there to light our ways.

L. T.

Men would be angels, angels would be gods.

POPE

*I saw an angel in the stone
and I only chiselled until it
was set free.*

MICHELANGELO

*The wind was bad, the rain pelted us
We were almost naked, famished, and lost
But inside each of us, an exquisite warmth
Gave us the courage to walk in step with the angel
Who guided us directly towards the promised land.*

*O! lyric Love, half angel and half bird
And all a wonder and a wild desire.*

R. BROWNING

*Thou fair-hair'd angel of the evening,
Now, whilst the sun rests on the mountains, light
Thy bright torch of love; thy radiant crown
Put on, and smile upon our evening bed!*

BLAKE

There were three tall angels above our heads
Three angels with white, supple,
  and transparent forms
Following the black cortège, tender, indulgent
Waiting for these honest peoples' souls.

L. T.

The young wanderers with prickly hearts
Belch out like dragons and make fun of angels
But these mischievous beings,
  who have known much worse
Protect them in spite of them,
  disguised as butterflies.

L. T.

The poor looks for wealth
and the rich for heaven,
but the wise one searches
for a state of peace.

S. RAMA

Bless the Lord, you angels of the Lord, sing praise to him and highly exalt him for ever.

THE BIBLE

Hope springs eternal in the human breast:
Man never Is, but always To be blest

POPE

Angels are so beautiful with their veils of light
I would like to travel their solar universe
Walk by their side towards the opened heavens

L. T.

Through the trees during the month of May
Diaphanous shadows drift
They are angels, cheerful angels
Dancing for us under the plane trees.

L. T.

Many people who came within a hair's breadth of death spoke of an extraordinary and soothing meeting with their angels, while most of them were told that "their time had not yet come".

Returning where I came from,
looking back or going forward
Today or yesterday,
it makes no odds
Since my angel is beside me
Every instant of my quest.

L. T.

Among the Powers, we find the angels of birth and death; they carry the consciousness and history of all humanity.

When the pure-hearted angels
Take me by the hand
I follow them silently
Life is tomorrow.

L. T.

To love angels
is to believe in beauty
To love beauty
is to believe in the absolute
To aim for the absolute
is to believe in the eternity.

L. T.

Music is well said to be the speech of angels.

T. CARLYLE

I had a long shiver
but I was not cold
I trembled for a moment
but I was not afraid
I was blinded by its intense light
And yet I saw everything more clearly than ever
before
When my angel came
to show me the way.

L. T.

An angel, robed in spotless white,
Bent down and kissed the sleeping Night.
Night woke to blush; the sprite was gone.
Men saw the blush and called it Dawn.

L. DUNBAR

While guardian angels are assigned to individuals, Principalities watch over groups of people. They are also called angels of integration.

We are all fascinated by angels, their beauty, their lightness, their proximity to the spirit world. By appealing to angels in our lives, we open ourselves to love and transcendence.

L. T.

Angels are bright still, though the brightest fell.

SHAKESPEARE